anythink

D0515583

21st Century Junior Library

Levels

By Katie Marsico

CHERRY LAKE PUBLISHING * ANN ARBOR, MICHIGAN

Published in the United States of America by Cherry Lake Publishing
Ann Arbor, Michigan
www.cherrylakepublishing.com

Content Adviser: Roger McGregor, Director, Hannibal Career and Technical Center, Hannibal, Missouri

Reading Adviser: Marla Conn, ReadAbility, Inc.

Photo Credits: Cover, ©Yuri Arcurs/Shutterstock, Inc.; page 4, ©auremar/Shutterstock, Inc.; page 6, ©Kkulikov/Shutterstock, Inc.; page 8, ©Blend Images/Shutterstock, Inc.; page 10, ©Kzenon/Shutterstock, Inc.; page 12, ©Terrance Emerson/Shutterstock, Inc.; page 14, ©pryzmat/Shutterstock, Inc.; page 16, ©Seregam/Shutterstock, Inc.; page 18, ©Pavel K/Shutterstock, Inc.; page 20, ©MJTH/Shutterstock, Inc.

LIBRARY OF CONGRESS CATALOGING-IN-PUBLICATION DATA
Marsico, Katie.
  Levels/by Katie Marsico.
    pages cm.—(Basic tools) (21st century junior library)
  Audience: K to grade 3.
  Includes bibliographical references and index.
  ISBN 978-1-62431-172-7 (library binding)—ISBN 978-1-62431-304-2 (paperback)—
ISBN 978-1-62431-238-0 (e-book)
  1. Levels (Surveying instruments—Juvenile literature. 2. Building—Equipment and supplies—
Juvenile literature. 3. Carpentry—Tools—Juvenile literature. I. Title.
  TA565.G74 2013
  621.9—dc23   2013008822

Cherry Lake Publishing would like to acknowledge the work of
The Partnership for 21st Century Skills.
Please visit www.p21.org for more information.

Printed in the United States of America
Corporate Graphics Inc.
July 2013
CLFA11

CONTENTS

A level helps a carpenter make sure furniture does not slope.

What Is a Level?

Look at the top of a table. Is it flat and even, or does it **slope** downward? What about the walls in your house? Do they stand straight? Or do they slant in all different directions? These and other surfaces must be perfectly **horizontal** or **vertical**. People use tools called levels to make sure they are.

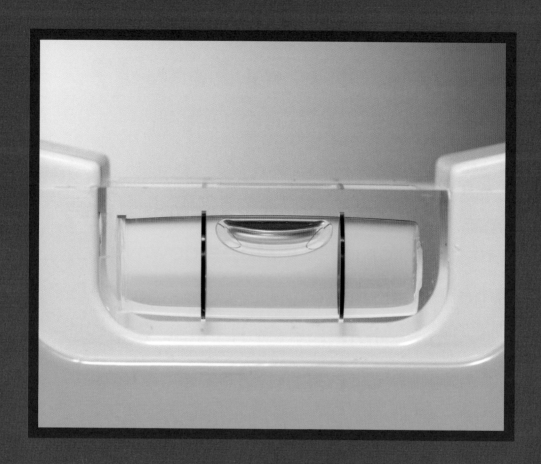

The liquid in a level is often green or yellow.
This makes the bubble easier to see.

Levels are usually made of a sealed glass tube. The tube is filled with liquid. An air bubble floats inside the liquid. The location of the bubble shows whether a surface slopes. This is important when someone creates horizontal, or level, surfaces. It is also important for vertical, or plumb, surfaces.

Levels can be useful when hanging a picture.

People rely on levels to do many different jobs. They use these tools to lay stones and bricks. Carpenters and builders work with levels, too. They use levels to make everything from furniture to houses. Some photographers use levels, too. They want to make sure a camera is level before taking a picture.

Ask Questions!

Talk to a carpenter or other craftsperson next time one visits your home. Ask about the ways the person uses levels.

Levels come in handy when someone lays floor tiles. The level helps make sure the tiles are even.

How Are Levels Used?

A person places a level on or alongside a surface. The person then looks at the level's air bubble. It often floats between a pair of lines. Hopefully, the bubble sits in the center of the lines. This means the surface is perfectly level or plumb.

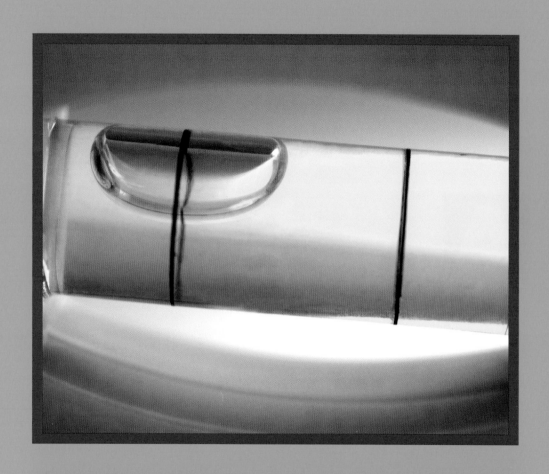

The farther a bubble is to one side, the more sloped a surface is.

The air bubble might be closer to one line. This means that the surface slopes. In this case, people usually make **adjustments** to the surface they are testing. Usually, they adjust the objects that support the surface.

Look!

Do your parents own a level? If they do, ask to take a closer look. Can you spot the air bubble?

A person checks that an object, such as a pipe, is plumb or level after making adjustments.

For example, maybe a tabletop is slanted. A carpenter might fix one of the table legs. Then the carpenter uses a level to test the surface again. The carpenter keeps working until the bubble lands in the center of the lines.

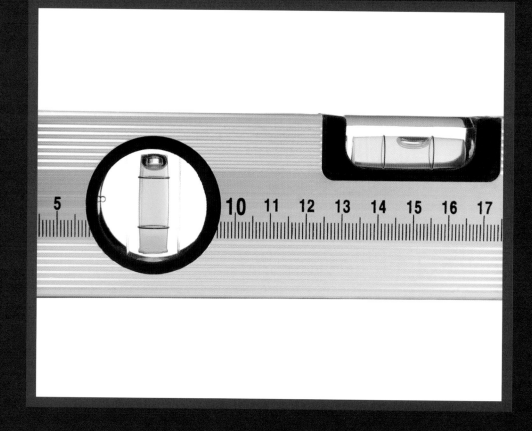

A level with measurement markings can also serve as a ruler.

Different Kinds of Levels

S ome levels are filled with liquid and an air bubble. These are called spirit levels. People sometimes use spirit levels in **construction**. Not all spirit levels are exactly the same. Many are made with long tubes that look like rulers.

Laser levels help someone make sure the floor, wall, or other object is level or plumb as it is being built.

A bullseye level has a circular container. Its bottom is flat. Bullseye levels are useful with broad, flat surfaces, such as kitchen counters. The level helps check that the counter is perfectly horizontal in every direction.

People often use laser levels with construction projects. These levels make a dot or line of light. Workers use the light as reference. It helps them keep everything level or plumb.

Have you ever tried cooking or eating on a tilted surface? It would be pretty messy!

Can you imagine life if levels did not exist? Food would slide off tables and counters. Pictures would fall off walls. Walking across the floor could feel like climbing a hill. These tools help people create the horizontal and vertical surfaces that shape the world we live in!

Create!

What would your house look like if people had not used levels to build it? Draw a picture of it. Show how furniture and other objects inside would appear, too!

GLOSSARY

adjustments (uh-JUHST-muhnts) movements or changes made to something

construction (kuhn-STRUHK-shuhn) the business of building houses and other structures

horizontal (hor-i-ZAHN-tuhl) straight and level, parallel to the ground

slope (SLOHP) to slant or be at an angle

vertical (VUR-ti-kuhl) upright, or straight up and down

FIND OUT MORE

BOOK

Nelson, Robin. *What Does a Level Do?* Minneapolis: Lerner, 2013.

WEB SITES

eHow: How Does a Level Work?

www.ehow.com/how-does_4567367_a-level-work.html

Learn more about how people operate levels.

How Stuff Works: Level

http://home.howstuffworks.com/level.htm

Find out more about what levels do and how to take care of them.

INDEX

ABOUT THE AUTHOR

Katie Marsico is the author of more than 100 children's books. She lives in a suburb of Chicago, Illinois, with her husband and children.